50 Tips for Home Buyers

WILLIE KRUGER

HEMBURY
BOOKS

About the author

Willie Kruger is a two-time author and self-made millionaire who knows what it takes to transform finance from something you work for to something that works for you.

Like many people, Willie joined the workforce immediately after graduation. Soon, he had a steady job, a credit card, a comfortable flat and a new car. But what he didn't realise was that he also had a net worth of zero. He wasn't just working for his employer; he was also working for the landlord and the bank.

Lacking a financial education, Willie made poor investment choices focused on liabilities rather than assets. At 41, still with a net worth of zero, he decided to launch his own business. In less than five years, his manufacturing business employed over 100 people. Then, at 46, he started investing in properties – 15 years later, he owned 38. By creating multiple income streams in the form of rent, dividends and interest, Willie established a passive income capable of supporting his full, active life.

In *Money Mind* and *50 Tips for Home Buyers,* and through his coaching, Willie shares the simple fundamentals of building wealth and investing in your financial future. He lives in WA where he spends his free time with his grandchildren.

HEMBURY
BOOKS

First published by Hembury Books in 2026
hemburybooks.com.au
info@hemburybooks.com

Paperback ISBN 9781923765160
Ebook ISBN 9781923765177

Typeset by Lorena Susak

This advice is general and does not take into account your objectives, financial situation or needs. You should consider whether the advice is suitable for you and your personal circumstances.

NATIONAL LIBRARY OF AUSTRALIA

A catalogue record for this book is available from the National Library of Australia

Dedicated to Elise

Contents

Introduction

For most people, buying their home will be the transaction of a lifetime. Buying a home is an exciting journey towards having that special place to call your own. You can look forward to adding your personal touch and creating your own unique haven.

It is also a considerable commitment, both financial and long-term. No wonder doubts often creep in when the offer to purchase is presented. How can you be sure you're making the right choice? Are you overpaying? Can you afford it? Are there contractual issues? Did you take all your needs and circumstances into consideration?

The purpose of this book is to remove the doubts and help to navigate your home-buying journey with confidence. There is no such thing as the perfect house, but you can use these 50 tips to help you find the home that's perfect for you.

I want your home-buying experience to be a happy journey. Some of the tips may seem a bit harsh. The idea is not to scare you, but to make you, as a potential buyer, aware that there are pitfalls and legal obligations that become reality the moment you sign the offer to purchase.

The ideas in the book are easy to understand and will help you:

- To be in control of your emotions. When decisions are based on emotions, logic and calculated decisions often take a back seat.
- Not to pay more than the median price and to remove the fear that you may be making a poor investment.
- Buy well within your budget.
- Make informed choices around all the practical issues.
- Be aware of the contractual commitments.

WHEN IS THE RIGHT TIME TO BUY A HOME?

From a financial point of view, you may be in a good position to buy if:

- Your credit score is good.
- You have managed to save for a deposit.
- Your debt is manageable.
- Your rent is rising year-on-year.

One of the most significant reasons to buy a home is to build long-term wealth. Equity grows as the loan amount decreases. Think of your home as an appreciating asset.

- Before you buy, investigate suburbs with a history of positive growth. Check out the price trends and sales on real estate websites.
- A well-maintained home and a lovely garden command a higher selling price.
- Your home can also earn extra income, for example by renting out a granny flat.

The goal of a successful home investment will be to ensure that you don't overpay or pay more than the average price for the suburb.

Home ownership requires you to think long-term. Owning your home is a form of forced saving. Home ownership is not only a low-risk investment, but also an integral part of owner's wealth and retirement plan.

WHICH HOME IS BEST SUITED FOR DAILY AND LONG-TERM NEEDS?

The right home must offer a balance between privacy, community, security and practical issues. You can also choose between a freestanding home, semi-detached, single or multi-storey, flats, apartments and many more. Four things to consider:

1. **List your needs.** Must-haves can be size, number of bedrooms or bathrooms, location and special needs. Nice-to-haves can be a pool, a view or an upmarket area.
2. **Prioritise** those things that are most important to you. This could be safety, lifestyle or perhaps being close to health care. The checklist is your handy tool.
3. **Future needs.** Will the children be leaving home soon? Perhaps you are considering working from home? Try to find a balance between immediate and long-term needs.

YOUR HOME, YOUR INVESTMENT

It is important to think of your home not only as a place of shelter, but also as an investment. A paid-off home is a great asset. 'Owning your home is a good investment' is a phrase that has stood the test of time. Real estate is less volatile than the financial markets.

In the old days, all roads led to Rome, but in modern times all roads lead to retirement. People are living longer; you can look forward to living 30 years after retirement. A paid-off home is then your greatest asset, especially during retirement.

Your wealth plan should include not only ownership, but also a plan to reduce the loan amount as soon as possible.

Two important items to keep in mind when you're home hunting:

1. **Choose the best suburb.** Neighbourhoods that constantly renew retain their value. Location is critical.
2. **Don't overpay.** Buying a the right price is an investment. If you overpay, the loan becomes a liability.

THE 50 TIPS CHECKLIST

You will find a checklist at the end of the book.

The 50 tips in this book are a guideline to help you to be prepared and have a clear understanding of your needs and obligations. This will help you buy with confidence and to strengthen your bargaining power.

You may not be able to find a home that ticks all the boxes, but you can at least make sure that the items that are most important to you are addressed.

Please note that items are not listed in any particular order. You must decide which items are most important to you.

Tips 1–5: Be prepared, financially and emotionally.

Tips 6–10: These items deal mostly with the offer to purchase. You need to understand your obligations.

Tips 11–40: These tips deal with the practical, day-to-day issues that you will have to deal with once you have moved in.

Tips 41–50: These are the circumstances under which it may be in your best interests to walk away from the deal. For example, if you feel the selling price is too high and there is an unwillingness or no room to negotiate.

Tips 1–5

Be well prepared

1. Get pre-approval from the bank or lender

Get pre-approval for your home loan. Talk to your bank or lender. What can you afford? Be informed about the different loan options, the loan amount that you qualify for, and the required monthly repayments. Also consider the transaction costs. Transfer costs, legal fees, building reports and registration fees are over and above the purchase price.

It is not easy to find the ideal home that will suit your budget and your needs. Loan pre-approval or pre-qualification is the first step in home hunting. Your application will also provide you with your credit score. Pre-approval will give you an idea of what you can realistically afford.

Make use of the various online calculators to help you to calculate your monthly repayments. Align the monthly repayments with your budget.

The bank or lender will check your credit score when you apply for a loan. A high score will ensure that the bank or lender will grant you a loan. Once the loan amount that you qualify for is confirmed, you can narrow down the areas and price range that will suit your budget. Avoid a situation where you fall in love with a property you cannot afford or that you will not qualify for.

Committing to the deal of your life without pre-approval and a budget is flying blind with your money.

2. Did you take all expenses into account?

Do your budget (also called the balancing act). This is your monthly net income minus expenses.

Ownership comes with ongoing monthly expenses. A budget will be your strategy to make sure that you can afford the home you fall in love with.

Determine the amount you can afford to pay towards the home loan each month. Take all costs into consideration. Ask for existing accounts for rates, electricity and water.

The word 'budget' is not meant to be restrictive. It is merely a tool you can use to take control of monthly spending. Once you know where the money goes every month, you can start planning your future:

- Ownership monthly costs: Monthly ownership expenses include home and household insurance, rates and taxes, levies, loan repayments, water and electricity. Add up all ownership and monthly living expenses. This will tell you what price range will be best suited for your budget.

- Organise your monthly living expenses. Use an app, a spreadsheet or a piece of paper. Compare income and expenses (inflow and outflow). Are you overspending? Is there something you can change immediately?
- Balanced lifestyle. Status and social proof are the main reasons many people live beyond their means.

The budget is your point of reference. It is income vs expenses, every month. If you need some guidance on how to manage your budget you can check out my book *Money Mind*. It is a handy tool that can help you to keep your finances and wealth plan on track, available on Amazon.

The author John C. Maxwell explains budgeting perfectly. 'A budget is telling your money where to go instead of wondering where it went.'

3. Will your home become an asset or a liability?

Your home can be an investment or a long-term liability. Your home becomes an investment when you can pay a little extra every month and reduce the loan period from, say, 25 years to 12 years or less.

Let's say you bought your home at age 35 and you've managed to pay off your loan by age 45. You can then live loan-free for the rest of your life.

Once the loan is paid off you can use the available balance to acquire a second property, or perhaps to start your own business. Leave some room in your budget to reduce the loan amount. It could well be the best investment you will ever make.

Flexi loans or redraw facilities give lenders access to surplus funds. The danger is that home owners often use surplus funds for emergencies or non-essential items.

Consider this. If you use the flexi reserve to buy a lounge suite, the repayments will add up to 2.5 times the initial price. And another thing: do you really want to pay off a lounge suite over 20 years?

Your home becomes a liability when you decide to use the saved (flexi) amount to buy furniture, cars or boats.

A loan will get you a home. To grow wealth, you need a plan and a bit of discipline.

4. Keep emotions under control

I know you're looking forward to your house-hunting experience. Searching for that ideal house where you can personalise your own space is an exciting time. And for most people, buying a home is a lifetime event and a large commitment.

Buying your home can be compared to getting married – a happy search-and-commit experience followed by the need to make sure it is a 'happily-ever-after' experience.

Inexperienced home buyers often sign the sales agreement without reading the fine print. Simply falling in love with the renovated kitchen and then signing on the bottom line is risky business. Don't let emotions override logic. It is important to have a clear understanding of the immediate and long-term commitments. Consider the following before you sign:

- Be aware that there are contractual obligations. Ask your lawyer to explain the fine print and ensure that your rights are protected.
- Double-check the monthly budget. Does it allow for the repayments plus ongoing costs such as insurance, taxes and maintenance?
- Is the asking price market related?

- Are there any hidden costs or defects? Most contracts lean towards the agent and the seller, for example, the 72-hour and no-warranty clauses.
- Did you allow for all the immediate expenses, which may include moving costs and new furniture?
- Have you considered all the practical issues? Tips 11 to 40 are a handy guide.
- Are your rights protected if you change your mind?

Buying a home is a huge commitment. Make sure that you commit to a fair deal, based on a rational approach. To do that, you need to stay focused, set your boundaries and tick the important boxes. Emotional decisions can often lead to buyer's remorse or regret at a later stage.

First impressions, fear of missing out and many other factors are emotional triggers. The emotions vs logic dragon is always there. Yes, by all means, love your new house, love the kitchen, but keep a cool head.

Take your time before you sign.

5. Beware of clever sales talk

Let me start off by saying I have nothing against estate agents. They know the area and prices and they can connect you, the buyer, with a home best suited to your needs and budget.

Buyers must, however, realise that the smiling agent is not your friend. The offer to purchase is a business transaction. It is a legal document that contains obligations, time frames and penalties.

Clever sales talk often generates emotions and subconscious commitment. Here are a few examples:

- **Overselling:** Overstating features and benefits.
- **Sales pressure:** 'I don't want you to miss out.'
- **Manipulation:** 'As you know, we have to accept the first offer.'
- **Overstating value:** 'An investors dream' or' endless possibilities.'
- **Misleading words:** Using words like 'cosy' instead of 'cramped.' A questionable location is often referred to as a 'hidden gem.' They say 'low-maintenance' rather than 'small.'
- **Real estate jargon:** Does 'it's a blank canvas' mean you can personalise it, or does it mean it needs a lot of effort to fix?

The checklist is a useful tool to keep a rein on emotions and assist you in making an informed and confident decision.

This is very important: You, the buyer, will be paying a third of your income every month for the next 20 or 25 years. In a real estate transaction, the buyer is the most important person. So don't be shy to:

- Check size, layout and quality. Check and double-check.
- Ask questions. Why is the seller moving? Are there defects or other issues? Talk to the neighbours.
- Take a couple of days to calm your emotions.

Take your time. Don't rush. Don't feel pressured. Once the offer to purchase is signed it is a legally binding document. Conditions can be changed at a later stage, but only if the seller agrees to it.

Listen to the sales talk, but use the 50 tips
to make up your own mind.

Tips 6–10

Take note of your rights and obligations

6. There are obligations under an offer to purchase

The offer to purchase is a legal setting of the rules between you as the buyer, the seller, and the real estate agency.

Please note: there is no common interest. The seller wants a high price, the agent wants commission, and the buyer must balance their needs and budget. Each party is chasing its own interests.

The contract conditions set out each party's obligations, time frames and what happens if any party fails to comply with the terms.

Real estate transactions require a written contract. Anything 'I said' or 'you said' will not be considered. Once the offer to purchase is signed, you cannot withdraw without incurring penalties.

If the buyer decides to pull out, they may lose the deposit, and they may also be held liable to for the agent's commission.

Before you sign, ask your lawyer to help you with the fine print. Understand all the clauses and time frames in the agreement. Calculate all the costs that will be for your account. Once you've signed you cannot add, omit or change any of the conditions if you change your mind.

You cannot have the house without any obligations.

7. The offer to purchase is not a friendly document

The offer to purchase is a binding agreement, meaning you, as the buyer, cannot cancel without incurring penalties. You need to include conditions (escape clauses) to protect you.

Watch out for the 72-hour clause. Also called the continued marketing clause, this allows the seller to continue marketing the property even after accepting your offer. In the case where the seller can secure a better offer, the first buyer has 72 hours to fulfil the suspensive condition, or let time lapse, meaning the first offer is cancelled.

Additional costs for the buyer. The agent's commission is paid by the seller. But the buyer could be liable for advertising, contract and administrative costs. You can negotiate all these costs before signing.

Default clauses define remedies in case of breach or failure to fulfil. The default party may be liable for penalties and damages, including the agent's commission and conveyancing fees.

Before you sign, make sure that:

- You can afford the property.
- The selling price is market related.
- You agree with the date for occupation and any occupational rent.
- You include terms and conditions that will protect you.

A contract is an exchange of value. Make sure the scale is balanced before you sign.

8. Never sign a blank contract

The contract you sign is a complex document, perfected over many years. All the information relating to the agent, the seller and the property must be filled in before you, as the buyer, sign the offer to purchase.

The offer to purchase contains several default clauses related to events and time frames. Contract clauses spell out the consequences if the buyer fails to pay or is in breach of any their obligations.

You will be signing for the deal of your life. Take your time before your sign, and act in your own best interests:

Never sign a blank contract.

- Don't rely on consumer protection legislation.
- Ask the conveyancer or your attorney to draft or check the offer to purchase before you sign.
- In the case of a sectional or strata title, check out the levy and rules related to maintenance and parking spaces.

There is no rule about who should sign first. If you, as the buyer, sign first you will lose all your bargaining power, and there is no guarantee that the seller will sign. They may keep on marketing the house to achieve a better price.

The agent will present you with a standard offer to purchase. It is not tailor-made for your specific needs. Before you sign, ask your lawyer to make sure that:

- All the details related to the property, price and seller's details are correct.
- You agree with occupation date and any occupational rent.
- Suspensive conditions that will protect your rights if you change your mind are included.
- Clauses like the without warranty and 72-hour clauses are removed.
- The seller is in possession of the original title deed and the local council plans.

Once you have signed a blank contract, all you can do is hope for the best.

9. Are there approved building plans?

Sometimes people only discover years later when they want to sell their home that additions were made without approved plans. The local council may then refuse to accept unapproved additions, in which case they can levy fines and, in extreme cases, order that illegal structures be demolished.

Ask for the approved building plans. It is not a legal requirement for the seller to provide these, but it certainly is good practice. Bear in mind that the bank may require a copy of the approved building plans prior to approving your loan.

Additions like carports and sheds must be shown on the building plans. If there are discrepancies, it is a good idea to include a clause stating that the seller must, at their own cost, appoint an architect or draftsman to draw up 'as-built' plans for approval. The design and approval process may then cause substantial delays in the buying process.

My advice is to:

- Add a suspensive condition that gives the buyer the opportunity to withdraw at no cost if approved plans are not available or if the plans differ from what you see on site.

- Delete the without warranty clause. The clause may make the absence of building plans a latent defect, for which the buyer's legal recourse is limited.

No approved plans = No deal.

10. Certain items may not to be removed by the seller

Although a property is sold with fittings and fixtures, it is in your best interests to draw up a detailed list of items that are to remain in the house as part of the offer to purchase. The seller may not remove anything that is of a permanent nature.

Items that are nailed down, fixed or bolted to the structure are considered fixtures. These items can include cabinets, bookshelves, cupboards and bicycle brackets. A television, although fixed, is usually not included.

Items that provide shading. Blinds, awnings and curtain rods are regarded as permanent, but it is nevertheless advisable to list all these items as part of the agreement.

Garden and landscaping. Structures like verandahs and sheds, or anything that is planted or sown, is regarded as permanent.

Agree which items are included in the sale. Stoves and ovens are considered permanent. Other items like the fridge, washing machine, dishwasher and window coverings need to be agreed on.

Take photos of the garden, irrigation system, light fittings, ceiling fans, shelving and floor coverings. A detailed list will avoid later misunderstandings over small items.

As part of the offer to purchase, include a list with the exact descriptions of furniture, appliances, window coverings, shelving and pot plants that are included in the sale. Confirm that the value of these goods is included in the selling price.

List everything that is included in the contract,
so that you don't have to rely solely on trust.

Tips 11– 20

The total cost, not only the purchase price

11. Consider the total liability before you commit

Want to make an offer on a house? Be aware of the costs you will incur over and above the selling price:

- **Additional costs:** Transfer fees, loan registration and moving costs.
- **A professional inspection:** For peace of mind that you are make an informed decision. Any defects that are uncovered can then be negotiated as part of the selling price.
- **Administration fees:** If the agreement includes agent's contract and advertising fees, these will be for the buyer's account.

Look at the general condition of the house, garden, paving and security installation. Will you be able to live with the current condition of the paint, carpets and kitchen cupboards? Any repairs, upgrades or repair of unnoticed defects will be for the buyer's account.

Ask a professional to help you calculate the **total buying cost** (once-off plus ongoing) before you sign on the bottom line. Overspending can lead to a cycle of debt.

Ongoing costs are the monthly expenses for:

- Monthly loan repayments.
- Rates, taxes, and strata fees and levies for apartments or sectional title properties.
- Insurance for home and contents.
- Security systems.

When you sign for an account, lease or loan you are selling your future labour. Home loans create equity, and so it is wise that this is the only debt you have.

12. Patent and latent defects

Both the buyer and seller should be aware of their rights and responsibilities related to obvious and hidden defects.

Patents defects are visible defects such as cracked tiles, sagging paving, leaking gutters and broken roof tiles. The seller is not required to disclose patent (obvious) defects. The 'as is' clause will protect the seller against legal action in this regard.

Latent defects are defects that are not visible. These are usually only discovered when a professional makes an inspection. The seller is obliged to disclose items such leaks in the roof, rising damp and structural damage. The buyer will have legal recourse relating to defects not disclosed or deliberately concealed by the seller. The buyer will have to prove that defects were deliberately concealed.

Employing the services of an expert or professional to advise on visible and hidden defects is highly recommended. Such an inspection can be a condition of sale. Ensure that the compulsory property condition disclosure is properly completed.

Doing your due diligence before you commit will be much easier than trying to prove deliberate concealment at a later stage.

'As is' or 'with all faults' clauses mean 'It's your problem and your cost if you did not do due diligence.'

13. Ask for the latest local government accounts

A clearance certificate for land tax charges is a legally required document. No outstanding local government debts should be carried over to the new owner. This involves obtaining a rates clearance certificate from the seller or their agent.

As the new owner, you will then need to open an account with the local council and pay the required deposits. Owners of sectional or strata title properties are also required to pay a monthly levy. The levy covers ongoing operating costs.

Information on your local government bill includes the account number, billing period, previous and current balance, and total now due. The amount due will be for water, electricity, sanitation, waste removal and property rates.

Have a good look at the municipal valuation:

- The valuation on the monthly statement indicates what you will pay towards rates and taxes every month.
- You can compare the municipal valuation with the selling price.
- If the municipal valuation is too high, you will be overpaying on rates and taxes every month.

- If the selling price of the house is much higher than the municipal valuation, it may well be a red flag. Consider other comparable properties for sale, re-negotiate the selling price, or decide if it may be a good time to walk away.

The municipal account with be a reliable indicator of your future monthly expenses.

14. Transfer fees are for the buyer's account

There are more costs to buying a house than the purchase price. Transfer duties and loan registration fees will be added on to the purchase price. The conveyancing attorney is appointed by the seller, but the purchaser is responsible for the fees. Best practice is for the buyer is to appoint a conveyancy attorney before signing the offer to purchase.

Do not confuse transfer fees and transfer duty.

- Transfer fees are payable to the conveyancing attorney for services rendered to transfer the property for the seller to the buyer.
- Transfer duty (or stamp duty) is a tax levied for transfer of ownership.

The buyer should consider the total cost of the move:

- Conveyancing costs and transfer fees.
- Valuation fees the lender will charge to make sure that the property value covers (or exceeds) the amount you want to borrow.
- Loan registration cost. Banks charge a fee to initiate the loan and open a loan account.
- Moving costs. You may have to hire a moving company.

- Home insurance.
- Estimated costs of repairs, remodelling and possible security upgrades.
- New appliances, furniture and window coverings.
- Setting up utilities, such as water, electricity, internet connection and refuse bins.

Buying a new home is a huge investment. It is important to plan and budget, taking all the buying costs as well as the ongoing monthly expenses into account.

15. Is GST included?

In the case where the seller is not a GST vendor, transfer duties will apply. If the seller (vendor) is registered for GST then 10% sales tax is payable.

In the case where the buyer is also a vendor, the input GST can be claimed back.

Either GST or transfer duty is payable, but not both. As a buyer it is in your best interests to confirm that GST is included in the purchase price if applicable.

Agent's commission is paid by the seller. Estate agents are obliged to disclose commissions and fees. Estate agents' commission is usually calculated as a percentage of the selling price, between 1.5 and 3.5%. Usually, GST is not included in the agent's commission, which is not fixed by law. The seller can negotiate the percentage and ask for GST to be included in the percentage commission.

Don't accept vague terms like 'commission will be subject to the final agreed price.'

Additional charges for administration, professional photography and marketing must be clearly noted in the agency agreement.

Before you sign, ask your agent or attorney to list all costs in the offer to purchase that will be for the buyer's account. And remember, all prices and costs are negotiable, but only before you sign.

16. Registration and ownership

Ownership is an important consideration when looking at your new home. In whose name will the property be registered? Ownership holds all the dimensions of possession, protection, control and benefit.

When a couple chooses joint ownership, they in effect become 50/50 business partners, and the deal relies on a lasting relationship. Joint ownership means partners are equally responsible for the entire loan and repayments. Ask your lawyer to assist with a cohabitation agreement before you buy. It will provide details about responsibilities and what happens if the relationship ends. Being prepared makes it easier to manage unexpected or unplanned events.

An advantage of a joint loan is that you can combine your incomes and qualify for a larger loan amount. Joint loans make it easier for younger couples to enter the property market. Consider life insurance, it will provide the other with enough support in case you pass away or cannot work

If one of the partners has a low credit score, the home loan application may be rejected. The partner with the best credit score should then apply for the loan.

Business risks often require some protection or a shield against creditors. If you are a business owner, or perhaps you consider starting an own business, then setting up a family trust, may well be a practical option. It offers advantages related to tax and estate duty liabilities. Trusts allow for easy transfer of assets and business interests (continuity and succession planning).

You will need to seek professional advice regarding the costs and obligations of setting up a family trust.

'Co-ownership is the mother of all disputes' – Old Roman law.

17. Consider possible immediate improvements

It is recommended that you don't spend money on renovations until the property is registered in your name. Should the sale fall through, your money and effort will be lost.

Before you buy, list all the items that may need repairs or remodelling. Check out the quality of paint, gutters, floor finishes and ceilings. Open and close doors, cupboards and the garage doors. Flush the toilets. Do all the electrical outlets work? Is there insulation in the ceilings?

Estimate the cost needed to bring the home to an acceptable living standard. The cost of repairs can perhaps be negotiated to become part of the selling price.

Be careful of a home in poor condition. Home buyers often undertake extensive renovations. Upgrades often lead to overcapitalising. Market conditions, **not** the cost of upgrades, dictate selling price.

Personalised items like expensive carpets can even devalue a home if, for example, a potential buyer prefers laminated flooring.

Not all improvements will increase value; for example, replacing steel windows with expensive aluminium windows. Potential buyers may view windows as simply windows, and not distinguish between steel and aluminium. Buyers are more focused on room sizes and practical issues and may not pay attention to high-end fixtures like expensive ceiling fans.

First impressions, like the beautiful garden, an inviting entrance and perhaps a new garage door always create buyer's interest.

Consider the median price. What will your total investment be? Will the house price plus estimated cost of renovations exceed the average price for the area? Be mindful about improvements, especially if return on investment is important.

Don't underestimate the cost to upgrade from house to home.

18. Electricity, gas, solar and inverter batteries

It is a good idea to know what your monthly account will be for water, electricity, waste removal and land rates. This amount is over and above the monthly loan instalment, and you should allow for it in the monthly budget.

Ask the seller for a copy of the current accounts from the seller. If there are any outstanding balances, the council will not issue a clearance certificate. You can ask the seller to pay any outstanding balances before you sign. This will ensure that that are no delays in the transfer process.

A house with an existing solar installation and a gas stove may be first prize. In the case where solar was installed three or four years ago, the inverter battery may have to be replaced soon. Since this is costly item, consider making the replacement battery part of the negotiation process.

A solar installation combined with a battery will significantly reduce reliance on the electricity grid. Lower monthly electricity bills is not the only advantage. Safety and security remain intact because the battery will ensure that garage doors and alarms will remain active should there be outages.

Currently the situation is that often the is no current.

19. Is there space for a water tank?

A house with a water tank is a bonus:

- Harvesting rainwater for irrigation is an ongoing saving.
- Washing machines, pools, fish tanks – everything needs water.
- A water tank can reduce your water bill by 30% or more.
- If properly stored, water has an indefinite shelf life.

Consistent water supply is gaining importance as shortages and interruptions are becoming more frequent year-on-year, not to mention the rising cost of clean water.

Tanks can be filled by rain or borehole water. Where space is limited, tanks can be installed underground. Water from tanks can be purified or boiled for drinking purposes.

You can even fill a water tank from your gutters. In this case, you will need to install a filter to remove debris and a harvesting system to channel water from the gutters to the tank.

Water tanks, solar and security installations will improve your lifestyle and increase the selling price of your home in future.

Water is our most critical resource – no water, no life.

20. You get what you negotiate

With the pre-qualification amount in hand, you can offer and negotiate with confidence.

Everything is negotiable. Buy at the right price. Don't be shy to offer less. You get what you negotiate. Always ask yourself: If I have to sell this property tomorrow, will I get my money back?

Beat inflation by negotiating a 10% discount. Negotiate a lower interest rate with your bank, or use another bank. Insurance premiums, home loan interest rates and bank charges can all be negotiated. And don't forget to ask for a raise!

Don't overpay. Check out the suburb's median prices. Use Google. The property sites will tell you which areas show consistent growth. Make your offer subject to a valuation and inspection by your loan provider.

When you buy a house almost everything can be negotiated. This includes:

- Interest rate on the loan.
- Offer lower than the asking price.
- Add value to the price. Include window coverings, pot plants and the dishwasher.

- Ask the seller to lower the price if the garden, gutters and paint surfaces are in poor condition.
- Look for bespoke furniture or garden equipment that cannot be moved easily.
- Occupational rent can always be negotiated.
- Ask the agent to consider a lower commission.

The keys to success:

- Negotiate strategically.
- Keep emotions out of the process.
- Never share your budget.
- Know the limits.
- Don't lowball; unrealistically low offers can create disrespect and bring an end to negotiations.

Rule 1 of negotiating: Knowledge is power.

Tips 21–40

Practical day-to-day living conditions

21. Location is paramount

Location, location, location. The phrase has stood the test of time. The choice of location directly impacts daily lifestyle, resale value and the long-term growth potential of the property.

Most people value being close to amenities like schools, shopping centres and green areas. These days, more people prefer working from home. Safety, walkability and noise levels are strong considerations.

Anything you spend a lot of money on can be viewed as an investment, meaning it becomes part of your wealth-building plan. Location affects both value and desirability. A well-kept home is an appreciating asset. Your home could have investment potential or it could be used to yield consistent returns:

- Your home can generate monthly rent income.
- Land can be subdivided for development or rezoned for commercial use.
- A granny flat, parking or storage space can be rented out.

It's easy to get swept away by a modern kitchen or a huge entertainment area. But my advice is to never sacrifice features or layout for location.

Never say never. Location holds up when circumstances change. When the unexpected or the unplanned happens, the value of your home suddenly becomes vital. Location remains a smart choice. More than anything else, the house's location is the determining factor of its future value and the time it will take for it to sell.

When you're out hunting for your home, think of location as that one thing you cannot change.

22. Value your lifestyle and privacy

The final choice of your home may well be a compromise between location, practical issues and your preferred lifestyle. Narrow down the issues that are most important to you. It could be walkability or being close to medical facilities.

Privacy is not something to be overlooked. There is more to privacy than high fencing, security cameras and safe driveways:

- If you are living in an estate, the security company knows everything about you.
- High walls offer no protection from noisy neighbours, restaurants or busy roads. Noise pollution is not an easy matter to deal with.
- Be aware of possible visual intrusion from overlooking or high-rise developments.

Be mindful about sharing personal information when you make an offer. The best protection is to use an established real estate agency. It is common practice for estate agents to take photos and videos of the home for sale, inside and outside. Ask your agent to remove those images after the sale.

A town or urban planner can also advise you of future developments in the area. High-rise accommodation and commercial developments affect not only privacy, but eventually also the resale value of your property.

Privacy is one of those hidden factors that directly impact on lifestyle and eventually the selling price.

23. Roads and traffic affect everyday life

Houses that are for sale are generally not open for viewing during peak traffic hours. Do a dummy run of your daily commute to see how long it takes to get to work in the morning. Long commute times will add to both your frustration and your monthly expenses.

It may be convenient to be close to major roads and highways, but be aware of potential noise and pollution. Hooters, headlights, police and ambulance sirens all impact on quiet time.

WHAT TO WATCH OUT FOR

Busy roads require you to be extra careful with kids and pets. Dense traffic is not always safe for walking or cycling. Heavy pedestrian traffic can be a constant nuisance.

YOUR HOME, YOUR INVESTMENT

Location still tops the list for property performance. If you are looking for capital growth on your home, then a house close to busy roads is not recommended. The selling price of a house close to a busy road should be approximately 15% below the median price.

A HOME IN A CUL-DE-SAC IS A SOUND INVESTMENT

A house in a shorter street with a circular end offers less pedestrian traffic and noise. A cul-de-sac provides a safe area for children to play or ride their bikes. Cul-de-sac locations are highly desirable. A home in a cul-de-sac is a wise choice, not only for noise and safety, but also as a sound investment.

Roads, railways and highways are progress for some, but a nuisance for others.

24. Stormwater and falling leaves

Stormwater, overhanging trees and falling leaves often lead to spoiled relationships with neighbours. A neighbour cannot be held responsible for failing to clean up leaves that fall into your property, nor are you allowed you return the leaves. A friendly neighbourly chat should be your first step to finding a solution.

If you are interested in a low-lying property, it may be a good idea to find out if what happens if rain and stormwater flow down from the higher-lying property. The owner of a low-lying property must accept stormwater from the higher-lying property. The low-lying property cannot block the natural flow of water.

It is not permissible for an owner of a high-lying property to deliberately channel stormwater to a certain point. The owner of the lower-lying property will have legal recourse where the natural flow of water is deliberately increased.

My advice is to talk to the neighbours before you commit. Ask them, 'Are there any agreements or disagreements related to leaves, stormwater, or any other issues for that matter?' Communication creates respect and understanding.

Trees are part of our natural environment and deserve our tolerance. Falling leaves can be controlled by pruning overhanging branches. Enjoying the birds, bees and animals living there may be a better option that cutting down the tree.

Friendly relations with your neighbours is your first line of defence to resolve issues like stormwater, falling leaves and barking dogs.

You can change your friends, but not your neighbours.

25. Choose a north-facing home

Sunshine provides free natural light and heating during the winter months. In the Southern Hemisphere, the sun's path is predominately to the north, rising in the east and setting in the west. A well-designed home will have the living rooms and bedrooms facing north, enjoying the most direct sunlight during the day. As the house warms up during the day, heat will spread to other rooms.

Sunlight is a passive source of energy. Well-designed roof overhangs will reduce reliance on artificial heating in winter and keep indoor spaces cooler during the summer. Roof overhangs will not only save on electricity bills, but will also protect walls from damaging sunlight and rainwater.

Limited west-facing windows will reduce excessive heat and glare from the low afternoon sun.

The sun is low in winter and high in summer. Awnings and roof overhangs are essential building elements to reduce excessive heat in summer.

Apart from their aesthetic appeal, roof overhangs will protect your home from the elements. Gutters fitted to overhangs can collect water for storage and irrigation.

Roof overhangs and a wide north-facing elevation are hidden building elements that will increase lifestyle and selling value.

26. Is there enough storage space?

Storage space is not something to be ignored. Let's think of a few items that need storage space:

- Hobbies and collectables.
- Files and documents.
- Books and magazines.
- Photo albums.
- Suitcases.
- Garden equipment and tools.
- Spare clothes, blankets and pillows.
- Sports equipment like golf clubs.
- Boats, caravans and trailers.

Space-saving ideas, multifunctional furniture, under-stair storage and garden sheds are options available to increase storage space.

Bear in mind that creating storage space at a later stage will be for your account. Sheds, shelves and cupboards are expensive items.

You can use a checklist to make sure there is enough storage space to meet your needs. Plenty of storage means less clutter. Items to consider:

- A pantry for all the kitchen goodies.
- Under-stair storage for suitcases.
- Storage for sports equipment.
- Linen and clothing cupboards.
- A garden shed for tools and lawnmowers.
- Shelves for camping equipment.
- Cupboards or shelves for books and documents.

Many home buyers regard adequate storage space as a must-have.

Not sure why we keep stuff for 20 years before we throw it away or sell it. Choose to declutter. Less stuff means less to organise, less to store and less to clean.

27. Have a close look at the carpets and cupboards

Moving to your 'new' home? The truth is that the house you are buying could be 30 years old, or more. Some houses could easily be 100 years old. Unless you're building or buying in a new development, you are most likely buying a house where cupboards and fittings may well be past their useful life.

It won't do any harm to confirm the age of the house. It could be the date stamp on the building plans or perhaps the average age of houses in the suburb.

Check out the quality of carpets, doors and cupboards. Don't be afraid to open and close them. Are the drawers falling apart? Look for signs of damp. Open the cupboard doors under sinks. Are there signs of water damage?

What is underneath the new carpets? Do you notice any unevenness, sagging or creaking in the floors when you walk in the house?

Don't forget to:

- Open and close the garage doors and garden gates.
- Run the air conditioning system or split units. Make sure

heating and cooling happens in a reasonable amount of time.

- Arm and disarm the home's security system. Include the security company's contact details in the offer to purchase. All the access codes and remotes will have to be changed on the day you move in.

Don't underestimate the cost of replacing or upgrading interior finishes. Cupboards, flooring, sanitary and light fittings make up 35% of the total cost of building a new house.

28. What is the paint hiding?

The seller is obliged to disclose hidden defects, but in reality, sellers usually don't disclose them, and often cover them up. A fresh coat of paint can hide issues like rising damp as well as structural issues. Look out for leaks and signs of damp. Can you smell mildew? Is the new wallpaper hiding cracks? Most sales contracts include a *"As is"* clause stating that the buyer accepts responsibility for patent (visible) and latent (hidden) defects.

Latent defects can be described as flaws that cannot be identified despite a reasonable inspection of the property. Latent defects can also include things such as noisy neighbours and soil issues. The buyer can take legal action and claim damages or cancel the sale if a case of deliberate concealment can be proven.

For the buyer: Prevention is better than cure. Legal battles are costly and never a sure win. Make your offer subject to an inspection by a professional.

For the seller: The clause will not exempt them from liability for defects covered by a fresh coat of paint.

Are the finishes hiding something?

If the house is old but the paint is fresh and the carpets are new, it may well be a warning sign to take a closer look. Check for signs at wall edges and in corners.

Look for signs of a staged home

Is there a monster in the closet? Sellers often decorate to make the house more attractive for potential buyers. What are the wallpaper and pictures covering up? Is furniture placed in strategic places for a reason? Why the mood music? Is it a trick to dampen traffic sounds or noises from defective plumbing?

Don't take everything at face value. Getting caught by a new carpet or a coat of paint will only serve to spoil the home-buying experience. Get the expert in. Do the inspections. Don't leave anything to chance or hope that everything will work out fine.

29. Don't forget the roof and the pool

Look out for cracked or loose roof tiles and ridges. What is the state of side wall flashings and downpipes? Sagging gutters and broken fascias are all visible signs of neglect.

Sagging occurs mostly with tiled pitched roofs. The most common causes of sagging are overloading and damp that causes rot. Risk of collapse cannot be ruled out. If the roof is in a poor state, I would not necessarily walk away from the deal if all the other conditions are met. Any roof problem can be fixed.

The roof, flashings, fascias and gutters are visible items. In most cases, sagging will be clearly visible and may not be a latent defect, meaning you cannot later claim repair costs from the seller. If you suspect there are roof issues, ask for an inspection and a quote to repair from a qualified roofing contractor. The cost to repair can then form part of the selling price.

THE SWIMMING POOL

Are the pump and filter in good working condition? Listen for unusual noises. When was it last serviced? Is the pool light working? Is there a place where chemicals can be stored safely? The pool's finish must be free of stains, discolouration and rough areas. Check the pool deck for signs of cracks or sagging. How old is the pool? Vinyl liners have a limited lifespan; approximately 10 years.

Safety first. Check the pool gate and fence. Does the pool area comply with building safety requirements?

'Fix the defects before you sign' refers to safe practice to ensure that all defects are resolved before you sign. The seller must agree to fix defects or the cost of repairs must form part of the purchase price.

30. Flat roofs are synonymous with maintenance

Personally, I would never buy a house with a flat roof. Compared to pitched roofs, flat roofs can come with a long list of problems:

- Expansion and contraction from temperature fluctuations can cause cracks and damage to flashings.
- Flat concrete roofs are prone to heat build-up, which is then radiated into the house, leading to excessive cooling needs.
- Flat roofs and drains need constant cleaning to ensure that water is effectively drained from the roof.
- Ponding on flat roofs can cause all sorts of problems, including damage to waterproofing membranes, added weight, roof leaks and growth of algae and moss.
- UV damage means constant maintenance to waterproofing materials and flashings.
- Drainage is always a problem with a flat roof because of the slight slope compared to pitched roofs.

Flat concrete roofs: Need periodic maintenance of outlets, flashings and the waterproofing membranes.

Flat roof sheeting: Ponding, leaks, corrosion, rust, loose fasteners – the list is endless. Do yourself a favour, stay away!

Nobody likes constant maintenance and repairs. If you are considering a home with a flat roof, I would recommend that you ask for an inspection by a specialist.

Limited lifespan, less stability, heat absorption, gutter failures and waterproofing issues convince me to stay away from flat roofs.

31. Have a good look at the quality of the windows and doors

The kitchen and entertainment area are top of the list for most people, rather than giving much consideration to windows and doors. Defects to windows will not be considered to be concealed by the seller. The buyer is free to open and close doors and windows.

Basically, there are three types of doors and windows:

- **Steel:** Steel is strong and durable, but the paint and putty need periodic maintenance. Steel does not seal well against weather and noise. Cold in winter, hot in summer.
- **Timber:** Offers style and provides more insulation than steel windows. Prone to shrinkage, warping and swelling, mostly due to water ingress between the outside beading and the glass.
- **Aluminium:** Remains an excellent choice for home owners. Integrated rubber gaskets seal well against weather and noise. Aluminium windows can accommodate a wide range of glass types for protection against sun damage, noise, and heat transmission.

> Laminated glass is recommended for safety, as it will remain in place even if the glass is broken.

Look out for damp under windows and cracked windowsills. Poor sill details will allow water to seep into the walls, causing damage to plaster and paint under the windows.

Don't be shy to open and close all the windows and doors. Do all the locks, handles and hinges function properly? Stacking or folding doors are expensive items to service if they get stuck. Scratched glass, sticky windows, leaks, warp and corrosion are some of the potential issues with windows and doors.

It is important to confirm that the glass in the windows and doors complies with national safety regulations. Glass in doors, and in windows where the sill height is less than 500 mm, must be either toughened or laminated safety glass. Safety glass will always have a specific symbol to confirm compliance.

For your own safety, ask for a certificate of compliance to ensure that the glass complies with safety standards.

32. Taps and toilets may be past their useful life

Plumbing and electrical installations could well be at the end of their useful life if you're looking at a property that is 50 years old or more.

Open and close the taps. Flush the toilets. Are there potential issues? Bagging or rattling pipes are an indication of inconsistent water flow caused by damaged pressure valves. Slow drainage and odours may be a sign of potential blockages or venting issues.

Flush all the toilets to make sure they work well, meaning they have sufficient suction. The tanks must fill up in a reasonable time. Make sure that the valves shut off properly.

Run the water in the showers and sinks. Make sure hot water comes through in a reasonable amount of time.

Check the water pressure in the taps and especially the showers. Low pressure or rattling pipes are often indications of a hidden problem.

The best way to check if there is enough water pressure is to open a shower. Low water pressure can be a frustrating, especially if it is a supply issue.

Water leaks can easily be detected. If all the taps are closed and the water meter is still moving, it is proof of water leaks underground, in pipe ducts or in the roof. Water marks or mould on the ceilings is a telltale sign of a leaking water tank or cracked roof tiles. Corrosion and leaks around the tanks may be a sign that replacement will soon be necessary. You can ask the seller about their maintenance history.

Don't forget the shut-off valves. Where are they? Are they easily accessible and in good working condition? Water that cannot be shut off in a hurry during an emergency can cause serious damage.

If you have any doubts, ask a plumber to do an inspection. The plumber will also be able to report on the quality of the pipes, tanks and drains – those items you cannot easily reach or see.

33. Was the house built by a professional builder?

Many houses are built by owner-builders, who do not always have the skills and experience needed to manage the construction process. Building is a complex process of co-ordinating and supervising all the different building trades.

It's a team effort. Just as with a rugby or soccer team, success is the result of an effective team effort. In the same way, building contractors depend on a reliable team of competent sub-contractors assembled over several years.

The devil is in the detail. Construction relies on professional design and building to comply with proven threshold, windowsill, expansion joint, reinforcement and damp-proofing details, to name a few. Knowledge of surveying, site set-out, soil stability, and supervising specialised trades is essential to achieving acceptable quality standards and legal compliance. Owner-builders do not always have the specialist knowledge and experience needed to achieve acceptable quality standards.

Damp, loading, structural and quality issues could well be the result of an owner-builder effort. Latent defects due to lack of skills and craftmanship may only become evident after the sale.

My advice is: Don't buy someone else's problems. An inspection by a competent person will reveal quality issues and possible long-term maintenance challenges.

Look at the quality of the finishings, skirtings, cornices, plaster and the roof overhangs. The telltale signs are in the small details. If you have any doubts, ask the seller who built the house.

34. Adequate parking is crucial

Check out the garage and available parking spaces. Is there is enough dedicated parking space for your cars and any trailers or caravans, and for visitors?

Consider both current and future needs. For example, an adult child living at home while studying may need an additional parking space.

Homes with adequate parking will be easier to resell compared to a property with restricted or unsafe parking.

Vehicles parked outside in sectional title or strata schemes will be on common property. As part of the sales agreement, you can ensure exclusive parking rights through a written agreement. Ask the conveyancer to assist and protect your rights in this matter.

Shared driveways often lead to disputes related to parking space and access rights. If you have to rely on street parking, it may be subject to permit restrictions or competition from neighbours.

Adequate parking space, or the lack of it, is a practical issue that home owners have to deal with every day. If you can spot an opportunity to add extra parking space at a reasonable cost, it may be a great way to boost the value of your home.

In some areas, extra parking space can even be rented out to provide extra income.

Easy access and adequate and safe parking are without question items that should be high up on your checklist.

35. Slopes provide their own challenges and advantages

A sloping property offers unique design opportunities. Home buyers are prepared to pay extra for lifestyle and privacy. While homes built on a sloping or terraced stand are sought after, they do provide their own unique challenges:

- Gardening and landscaping.
- Stormwater and soil erosion challenges.
- Inclined driveways and steep front walk-ups.
- Restricted access and parking space.
- Complex sewage, drainage and irrigation systems.
- Many levels means climbing stairs all day, every day.
- And don't forget, 'the tallest tree catches the most wind.'

Dealing with multiple levels is not for everyone. You may need to hike three levels from the garage to the kitchen every day. You may even have to allow for the cost of a home lift.

A home on slope will come with its own challenges. Even so, a well-designed house on slope that combines practicality, landscaping and a stunning view will always command a higher selling price.

I'm not saying rule out a house on a slope. But weigh the pros and cons that you will have to deal with daily.

36. Advantages of a view

Land with scenic views often provides interesting opportunities for custom design. Multi-level living, cantilever structures, landscaping and blending in with the natural environment all create a sense of space and privacy. The architect will focus on the best use of the unique view. Combining design and an exclusive view will enhance lifestyle and increase a property's value.

A stunning view will add to both value and appeal. A house built on land with a view will be more desirable than one without, even though the building cost for a similar design is the same.

A view often adds status and prestige. You can enjoy a breathtaking sunset and the beauty of nature every day.

A view also creates that emotional connection with a property, making it easy to resell at a higher price.

Exposure to the sea offers its own challenges. Wind and weather conditions often restrict the use of outside entertainment areas. Salty air can cause rust and rot, which reduces the lifespan of building materials. But despite higher maintenance and insurance premiums, the demand for homes with a view remains high, and as such they command a higher selling price.

A beautiful view offers exclusivity and enhances lifestyle. A home with a view is more than a home; it is also a good investment.

37. Security cannot be ignored

To feel safe and secure is a basic human need. Home security to protect your family and belongings is a priority for most home buyers these days.

Have a good look at the surrounding areas and identify anything that could be a security risk. Being next to a park, busy roads or a house with a street-front garage can all be less safe. Undeveloped sites and possible future high-rise developments can impact on security and privacy.

Home security can be a mix of:

- Traditional items like high walls and steel security gates.
- Technological items like automated gates, electric fencing and alarm systems. A CCTV system enables you to connect remotely.
- Motion control security cameras can detect movement in outside areas and trigger the alarm system.

Does the house have a fireproof safe to protect documents and valuable items like jewellery or art collections from fire and theft? Pay a visit to the house after hours. Does the area feel safe? Are there adequate exterior lights and streetlights?

Have a good look at the existing security elements. Are the boundary walls high enough? Pedestrians can act as 'spotters' to identify empty homes. Are there hiding places?

Does the quality of doors, windows and burglar-proofing create a safe environment? An automated entrance gate and garage door will significantly boost home security. The difference between what is there and what you would need to install or build to feel safe will most likely be an immediate cost.

Talk to the neighbours and the neighbourhood watch. They will be able to share valuable information about crime in the area.

38. Floor plan, layout and dimensions

Proportions matter. If a room is too big, space is underutilised. If it's too small, a room can feel cramped. Often bedroom sizes are compromised for oversized entertainment areas. Rooms for similar activities should be linked together, for example bedrooms with bathrooms, and kitchen and dining areas.

Room size is critical for functionality and convenience. Is there space in the laundry for a washing machine and a dryer? Is there adequate storage space for sports equipment, books, suitcases, gardening and camping equipment? Houses with split levels should preferably have at least one toilet on each level.

Ask for the approved building plans. Room sizes and dimensions should be shown on the plans. Compare dimensions with your existing home. Will your furniture fit into the new house? Lounge and dining room furniture are expensive items to replace if these do not fit.

Check the orientation. Does the house feel warm or cold? Is there enough natural light coming in? What do you see when you look out of the windows? Privacy is important.

Think about your lifestyle and daily routines. Do you work from home? Do the kids need a study area? Are you mobile enough to cope with stairs and slopes? Are there separate areas for work, rest and play?

Walk around the house. Feel the layout and the connections between different areas. Think function, comfort and privacy, and that will be your ideal home.

39. Why do they want to sell?

Downsizing, a growing family, and moving closer to work or schools are all legitimate reasons for a house to be for sale. Don't be afraid to ask the agent, 'Why did the seller decide to move?' Gauge their urgency to sell. Financial issues or moving abroad may open the door to negotiating a better deal.

While the sellers are not obliged to disclose everything, you can probe their reason for selling by asking important questions:

- For how long did the previous owners live there? Ask for the sales history. If ownership periods are short, try contacting previous owners and see what they have to say about the neighbours, noise, security and traffic. Find out if there are underlying issues.
- How long has the house been on the market? Longer than three months means the house is most likely overpriced.
- Were any structural repairs made recently? Are the guarantees still in place? Can the seller be specific about the scope of recent renovations, repairs or upgrades?

Make a checklist of items that you are curious about. Ask the agent or the seller if there is anything you should know about the area. Are there any liens on the property? How did they arrive at the selling price? What do they love about the place? Ask the questions. Vague or evasive replies like 'not sure' or 'sort of' should raise a red flag.

When is the occupation date? A 'quick sale' may open the door to negotiate a better price. A sense of urgency may be a sign of underlying issues.

Buying a house is a major commitment. You deserve both peace of mind and to live happily ever after.

40. Is there an opportunity for value-adding?

Your house is not only a home, it is also an investment. Strategic improvements and renovations can substantially increase its value. Think about possible resale.

Potential buyers often walk away from a home with a scruffy garden, but they may also be walking away from a lucrative investment. Re-painting and a bit of landscaping will increase value and lifestyle.

High return on investment (ROI) renovations include energy-efficient installations and upgrades to functional areas like the kitchen and bathrooms.

Real estate with high ROI potential includes:

- Homes on land that can be subdivided and developed.
- Land that can be rezoned for business rights.
- Homes that have income potential from renting out a granny flat or storage space.
- Potential additions. For example, buying a two-bedroom house in an upmarket area and turning it into a three-bedroom house will add significant value.

If you're considering additions, it is best to ask for an expert's opinion on the renovation potential of the property before you buy. These include:

- Zoning regulations restricting coverage and height.
- Easements for right of way and drainage.
- Permissions relating to height, privacy and closeness that may be required from neighbours.
- Alterations to older houses are often limited by heritage restrictions.

Three factors that will create demand:

- Location.
- Family-size homes.
- Condition.

First impressions are lasting. When you're buying, look beyond the garden and the fresh coat of paint.

When you're selling, make sure potential buyers walk through a beautiful garden towards a neat entrance.

Tips 41–50

Red flags

The final 10 tips are about issues that should raise a red flag.

Under these circumstances you may consider walking away from the deal.

41. The suburb's median price is a key indicator

The median price is the price at which half the properties sold for more and half for less in a specific area. Visiting houses on show, using online valuation tools and obtaining professional appraisals are all options that you can use to ensure the selling price of the property you are interested in is market related.

THE AREA'S AVERAGE PRICE IS CRUCIAL

Will the selling price of your home plus the estimated cost of planned renovations exceed the average price of comparable properties in the area? Overcapitalising can devalue your home if the buying price plus the cost of renovations exceeds what the property is worth.

A high asking price is an indication that you may not be buying from a motivated seller. If the seller is not willing to negotiate, it may well be in your best interests to walk away.

What happens if you must sell tomorrow? Divorce, loss of a job or a health setback often forces people to sell their home a short time after buying. In this case, all expenses related to the sale and moving are lost money. There may also be a loan cancellation penalty. When you sell, all the costs related to agent's fees, compliance and clearance certificates will be for your account.

THINK 'INVEST' WHEN YOU'RE HOUSE-HUNTING

Top of the 'must-have' list is always location. It is the foundation of property value. There is no need to hurry as there will always be houses for sale. Take your time, research the area. Knowledge is power. Don't be shy to negotiate, and be on the lookout for motivated sellers.

An 'investment mindset' will make it easier to compromise between immediate and long-term needs.

Do the sums, compare total capital outlay with the average price in the suburb. Total capital outlay will be the:

- Purchase price.
- Transfer and bond registration costs.
- Moving costs (and possibly new furniture).
- Expenses required for immediate renovations and improvements.
- Possible security upgrades.

Buying below the area's median price will ensure you acquire both a home and an investment.

42. No escape clause

A suspensive condition will allow the buyer to cancel or withdraw from the offer to purchase under specific circumstances without incurring any cost or penalties. Examples of escape clauses include:

- **Sale of the buyer's property.** The buyer is given a 30- or 60-day period to sell their current home.
- **Subject to approved building plans.** The buyer is given the opportunity to verify that the on-site buildings and boundary walls match approved plans.
- **Subject to inspection.** If an inspection reveals poor quality, stormwater issues or structural defects, the buyer is given the opportunity to withdraw.

Escape clauses mitigate risk and help the buyer to navigate unforeseen issues and circumstances without facing legal repercussions.

Bear in mind that an escape clause will only allow you to cancel under pre-defined conditions; in this case, your suspensive conditions. It is not broad or blanket protection if you decide to exit the contract.

Watch out for seller escape clauses. For example, the 72-hour clause will allow the seller to continue marketing the property after accepting your offer. This clause gives the seller 72 hours to find a higher price, in which case the seller can cancel the original agreement and accept the better offer.

Ask your trusted lawyer for protection against unforeseen events.

My advice is: No escape clause = No deal.

43. The 'as is' clause

Most sales agreements aim to sell the house as it stands, meaning the property is sold 'as is.' As the buyer, you agree to accept the house in its present condition, including patent and latent defects.

This offers protection for the seller, although it is not blanket protection. The buyer will have legal recourse in cases where hidden defects are discovered within a reasonable time. The onus is then on the buyer to prove the defects where deliberately concealed or not disclosed by the seller. Deliberate intent is tough to prove. In most cases, buyers will just have to accept that they bought 'as is.'

The 'as is' clause proves my point that real estate sales contracts lean more towards the seller and the agent than the buyer.

My advice is to remove the clause all together. If they refuse, walk away, or if you still want to proceed, add the following suspensive conditions:

- The sale is subject to an inspection by a professional.
- The sale is subject to receiving approved plans, and further, that the plans match all structures and boundaries in detail.

- The seller has the original title deeds. Title deeds provide valuable information related to rights, access and building restrictions.

MANDATORY DISCLOSURE

Ensure the seller discloses all known defects or conditions related to the property, and that the mandatory disclosure is attached to the offer to purchase before you sign.

If the roof leaks with the first rain, it also leaked with the last rain. The seller must disclose hidden defects or face legal consequences.

44. No cooling-off period

A cooling-off period refers to the period following the date on the offer to purchase, usually about five working days, that the buyer can cancel without incurring any penalties. Properties bought at auction or from companies and trusts do not automatically have a cooling-off period.

The law around cooling-off periods is complicated, and you should not rely on consumer protection legislation to get you out of a contract. Once you've signed the offer to purchase, it becomes an agreement of sale, and it is legal and binding.

The best way to protect your hard-earned savings:

- Never sign a blank contract.
- Never sign more than one offer to purchase in the hope that one will be accepted.
- Unless it's true, don't use 'not able to get finance' as an excuse. The seller has a right to confirm this with your bank.
- Ensure that the offer to purchase allows you a five-day window during which you can cancel without incurring penalties.
- Never sign before your trusted lawyer has checked all the clauses and conditions.

Protect your rights (and pocket) by including more than one suspensive condition, for example; the sale is subject to:

- Sale of buyer's current home, and by what date.
- Loan approval, and by what date.
- Defects and maintenance issues are revealed in an inspection report.

If any of the suspensive conditions are not met, the contract will lapse.

It is not possible for suspensive conditions to cater for all events.

Use the checklist, do the budget, get pre-approval, research the market, let your lawyer help you – and do all this before you sign.

The best cure is to make sure.

45. Existing buildings and the approved plans differ

The seller must disclose non-permitted construction and additions. Failing to disclose can have legal consequences. Additions require plan approval, inspections and, often, permission from neighbours. Local authorities can issue an order for non-permitted structures to be demolished.

It is worth noting that the seller is not legally required to submit approved building plans. It is, however, the buyer's right to ask for the plans.

Most offers to purchase are signed without the building plans attached. The buyer should then include a suspensive condition that the offer is subject to:

- Approved (stamped) building plan to be submitted for inspection, and by what date.
- The right to cancel if plans are not available or do not resemble the actual layout on site.

You don't want to find out at a later stage that the house and the building plans don't match. It may be too late to cancel the deal. You will then have to appoint an architect or draftsman to draw up as-built plans for approval. Then there is an added risk that additions may not be approved due to zoning issues, encroachment or easement restrictions.

Swimming pools need approval to ensure they comply with safety regulations.

Building close to boundary lines or double-storey constructions that may impact on privacy will need consent from neighbours.

If plans don't match what is on the site, or there are no approved plans, it may well be in your best interests to walk away.

46. Boundary issues can become a real concern

It is important to check if boundary walls comply with the regulations. Fences and solid walls are subject to building regulations, which are specific about height restrictions and structural integrity. . Most home buyers play a guessing game with boundary walls. A small investment in a registered surveyor will reveal exact information related to property size, restrictions and possible encroachments. Issues with falling leaves, overgrowth and overhanging trees can usually be resolved through a friendly neighbourly chat. Encroachment, for example by installing a fence that overhangs half a metre into the neighbour's yard without prior permission, can become a contentious issue.

A fence, structure or a road partially on your property is a violation of your rights. Boundary walls are shared property. Neighbours need permission before they can attach or demolish anything.

Boundary disputes are complex issues to resolve. Avoid nasty surprises and make your offer subject to a boundary inspection. Ask the owner, speak to the neighbours and find out if there are any ongoing disputes. Don't let the house cost you more than it should. Check and verify everything with the proverbial fine-tooth comb.

Be extra careful when you are viewing a property with a shared driveway or shared parking spaces. You will also be sharing responsibilities related to access, maintenance and repairs. Absence of a clear agreement with the neighbours can often lead to misunderstandings and disagreements.

Better to walk away from the deal if you suspect that there are disagreements with neighbours related to boundaries or shared spaces.

47. You feel pressured to sign

Agents are experts at exaggerating features and keeping quiet about negative details. They have many tricks up their sleeves to clinch the deal. Be aware of clever sales tactics. Buy time; that's the one thing we can all afford!

One way to overcome emotional decisions is to delay commitment. Negotiate a cooling-off period. 'Yes madam, it looks good but give me a day or two to think about it.' Have another look at the numbers. Do your own research. Are there other options? Get a second opinion.

Is the agent or seller unreasonable, unapproachable or inflexible? If you find that there is no room to negotiate the selling price and fees, it may be a good time to move on.

Common sales tactics include creating a false sense of urgency, for example, stretching truths about buyers' interest or multiple offers. Even creating high expectations like 'this property will be worth double in ten years' time.' Don't fall for creative wording like 'charming' and 'cosy.' Be wary if they agree with everything you say. The most effective sales tactic is to play on your emotions: 'It won't be easy to find another one that will fit all your needs.'

If you are anxious or feel rushed or pressured to sign, it may be in your best interests to back down. Take two days to calm your emotions. Talk to your lawyer, and make sure you understand all the details and obligations. Check the median price again. Compare the house with your lifestyle and priorities.

Sales pitches and tactics often create a sense of urgency to commit. Be prepared with your own lines: 'We're not in a rush to buy,' or 'I'm not sure if it exactly fits our needs,' or perhaps, 'This might be a bit over the budget.'

Unfortunately, you will have to listen to the sales talk, but do your own sums and make up your own mind before you sign on the dotted line.

Compare what you saw with your priority checklist. Does the house tick all the right boxes? Buying a house is a big deal and a long-term commitment, so keep a cool head.

48. Unresolved title issues related to ownership

Before you sign, ask for the title deed. This is a key document in the home-buying process. Without a valid title deed, transfer of the property cannot happen.

The title deed reveals valuable information related to:

- The full name and identity of the registered owner.
- The date and purchase price of the previous transfer.
- Restrictive conditions related to additions, zoning, subdivision and use of the land.
- Registered easements that may restrict your ability to build or make changes to the land.
- Possible commitments to a home owner's association.
- The size, boundaries and exact location of the property.

Unresolved property title issues can delay or even prevent transfer of the property into your name. Title deeds can be rejected by the relevant registry for several reasons, including:

- Public record errors, lost or misplaced deeds.
- Unpaid or unreleased mortgages.

- A lien against the property. The lien holder can hold or sell the property to recover debt.
- Unpaid property rates. The seller must provide a clearance certificate.
- Unclear boundaries and boundary disputes.

Find out if there are any ongoing legal issues that could potentially delay transfer of the property you are interested in, for example:

- The property forms part of a deceased estate.
- The property forms part of a contested divorce settlement.

Consider all restrictions and easements in the title deed before you buy, as it could impact on the value of the property.

49. What happens if you uncover hidden defects?

Don't miss out on the perfect home. Make your offer, but make it subject to a professional home inspection. If the inspection reveals defects, you will need detailed descriptions, photos and videos by your architect or engineer to support your withdrawal from the offer.

You're not an expert. As the buyer, you are more focused on practical day-to-day issues such as layout and room sizes. A professional home inspection is a practical option you can use to avoid costs and frustration at a later stage.

Patent defects are the buyer's responsibility. Sagged paving, cracked tiles and glass are obvious or plain-to-see items. As the buyer, you will have no recourse against the seller for these.

Don't be fooled. The 'as is' clause protects the seller. The buyer cannot deduct repair costs from the selling price or withhold occupational rent.

And the agent? The agent's responsibility is limited to inspecting and listing obvious defects, and obtaining a list of latent defects from the seller. You cannot cancel the sale or hold the agent responsible if you discover defects at a later stage.

The sales agent may present a pre-listing inspection report (or sellers report) as part of the offer. This report promotes transparency and reveals the exact condition of the home to the buyer.

If six months after transfer, the roof leaks and cracks appear in the walls, can the buyer claim damages? Only if the seller did not disclose or knowingly concealed them. Deliberate concealment is expensive and hard to prove. You'd be better off doing your due diligence beforehand.

'Subject to' is a suspensive condition. In this case, the offer to purchase will only become legally binding when the home inspection finds that there are no defects, or the report highlights minor repairs which may well be acceptable.

50. Bank's appraisal comes in below the price in the offer

The bank's appraisal will determine the property's fair market value. The property you buy will act as collateral against the loan.

THE BANK APPRAISAL CAME IN LOW

It could well be that the bank did not take appreciation or home improvements into consideration. What can you do if the assessment is below the selling price in the offer?

- You can increase the deposit to make up for the difference.
- You can ask the bank to take a second look.
- Ask another bank and pay for an alternative appraisal.
- Negotiate. A reasonable or motivated seller may choose to lower the selling price rather than lose the sale.

Do not end up underwater on your mortgage (meaning the house is worth less that you owe on the mortgage). If the selling price is higher than the bank's valuation and there is no room for negotiation, it may well be in your best interests to look for alternative properties for sale.

It is important to include the suspensive clause 'subject to bank appraisal.' If the appraisal comes in low it will give the buyer the option to negotiate a better price or walk away, without incurring any penalties.

Bear in mind that you are not only buying a home; you are also investing in your future and your retirement plan. The two golden rules of investing:

- Do your research and make sure you do not overpay.
- Who needs financial stress? Do the budget and buy affordably.

If you can do that, you may be able to pay off the mortgage in, for example, 10 years. Now you can live there for free, no more monthly rent or loan repayments!

If the price is too high, walk away. It is not guaranteed that the value of your house will appreciate, or that a greater fool will someday come along and pay more for the same thing.

Now that you are a home owner

Your home, your investment. Renting means you may have to move if the lease is not renewed. Ownership provides stability and an opportunity to grow equity, even for the average earner.

REGULAR MAINTENANCE PRESERVES VALUE

Home ownership involves constant maintenance. Owners should allow for approximately 2% of the home's value for annual insurance and maintenance costs. Maintaining the house, pool and garden is a monthly expense.

Maintenance is the process of keeping your home in good condition. Home insurance may cover the cost of damages and expenses such as water damage caused by broken water tanks.

Preventive maintenance like regular pest control and checking the roof, flashings and waterproofing will prevent expensive repairs at a later stage.

Corrective or reactive maintenance relates to unexpected items like a broken hinge or pane of glass.

Cosmetic maintenance is when we enhance the house's visual appearance, such as by landscaping or painting.

Health and safety maintenance involves, for example, installing a first aid kit, fire extinguishers or a bathroom extractor fan to prevent black mould.

Seasonal maintenance can include trimming trees and cleaning gutters before the rainy season.

KNOW YOUR NEIGHBOURS

Establishing friendly relations with neighbours will make it easier to resolve issues like falling branches. Neighbours can keep an eye on your home when you're away, water plants and even care for your pets.

Nothing stops you from meeting the neighbours before you buy. They are also a potential goldmine for firsthand information about security in the area and other potential issues.

Ask the neighbours:

- Did they know the previous owners?
- How long did they live there?
- Did they complain about anything?
- Why do they enjoy living in that area?

People like to talk. Neighbours will gladly share information about junk cars, overgrown lawns and noise in the area.

Meet the neighbours before you make the offer. It may well be the make-or-break in your decision to commit.

WILL ADDITIONS OR UPGRADES WILL BE REQUIRED?

Do the sums before you commit. Compare the home and floor plans with your needs. Will additions or renovations be required? If this is the case, you should consider comparing the selling price plus renovation costs to the area's median price.

Upgrades often lead to overcapitalising. When the purchase price plus the cost of additions exceeds resale value, you will be in a loss situation if you have to sell.

The cost of upgrades is often underestimated. Apart from the building costs, you may have to employ the service of an architect and an engineer. Plan approval is required before any site work can commence.

Upgrades take time. Design and plan approvals take time. Also bear in mind the construction time, disruption and possible security issues while building work is in progress.

Alteration is better than making additions. A larger house where you can modify spaces is often a better choice than making additions to a small house.

It is not easy to manage the dividing line between adding value and overcapitalising.

LET'S BE HONEST, MONEY IS IMPORTANT

Financial literacy is an asset in your bag. Understanding the financial components of budgeting, investing, borrowing and taxation is the first step towards creating wealth and moving away from debt. Decision-making skills will help you to weigh options and make informed choices that will align with your short- and long-term financial goals.

I hope that your new home will be more than a house, and will also be part of your long-term plan. Equity grows as the loan amount decreases. As with any type of investment, timing is everything. Buy low, sell high – and avoid a situation where you must sell in a hurry.

IS YOUR HOME AN ASSET?

The argument is academic. But for most people, home ownership is part of estate planning. A paid-off car and home when you retire is a great asset. A paid-off mortgage remains a high priority for many investors. Once you are a home owner, you can leverage the benefits to increase value, grow equity, and even look out for opportunities to create extra income.

BUYING YOUR HOME IS AN EXCITING EVENT

Use the checklist to create your own wish list. The guidelines in this book will help to navigate the buying process with confidence. Planning carefully, viewing many homes and having a good understanding of the buying process will ensure that you find a home that truly makes you happy.

If you do decide to buy, I welcome you to home ownership, and may your new home be filled with love and laughter.

Your checklist

- Get pre-approval from the bank or lender
- Did you take all expenses into account?
- Will your home become an asset or a liability?
- Keep emotions under control
- Beware of clever sales talk
- There are obligations under an offer to purchase
- The offer to purchase is not a friendly document
- Never sign a blank contract
- Are there approved building plans?
- Certain items may not to be removed by the seller
- Consider the total liability before you commit
- Patent and latent defects
- Ask for the latest local government accounts
- Transfer fees are for the buyer's account
- Is GST included?
- Registration and ownership

- Consider possible immediate improvements
- Electricity, gas, solar and inverters?
- Is there space for a water tank?
- You get what you negotiate
- Location is paramount
- Value your lifestyle and privacy
- Roads and traffic affect everyday life
- Stormwater and falling leaves
- Choose a north-facing home
- Is there enough storage space?
- Have a close look at the carpets and cupboards
- What is the paint hiding?
- Don't forget the roof and the pool
- Flat roofs are synonymous with maintenance
- Have a good look at the quality of the windows and doors
- Taps and toilets may be past their useful life
- Was the house built by a professional builder?
- Adequate parking is crucial
- Slopes provide their own challenges and advantages
- Advantages of a view
- Security cannot be ignored

- Floor plan, layout and dimensions
- Why do they want to sell?
- Is there an opportunity for value-adding?
- The suburb's median price is a key indicator
- No escape clause
- The 'as is' clause
- No cooling-off period
- Existing buildings and the approved plans differ
- Boundary issues can become a real concern
- You feel pressured to sign
- Unresolved title issues related to ownership
- What happens if you uncover hidden defects?
- Bank's appraisal comes in below the price in the offer

www.ingramcontent.com/pod-product-compliance
Lightning Source LLC
LaVergne TN
LVHW100326210926
848480LV00003B/1266